To dear Barbara —

Love from

Colleen

**PINK FREUD**

## Other books by Tohby Riddle

*Dog and Bird See the Moon*

*Irving the Magician*

*What's the Big Idea?*

*The Singing Hat*

*The Great Escape from City Zoo*

*The Tip at the End of the Street*

*Fifty Fairies You Ought to Know About*

*The Royal Guest*

*Arnold Z Jones Could Really Play the Trumpet*

*A Most Unusual Dog*

*Careful With That Ball, Eugene!*

# PINK FREUD

## Tohby Riddle

PENGUIN BOOKS

For Ivy and Archer – who make me laugh.

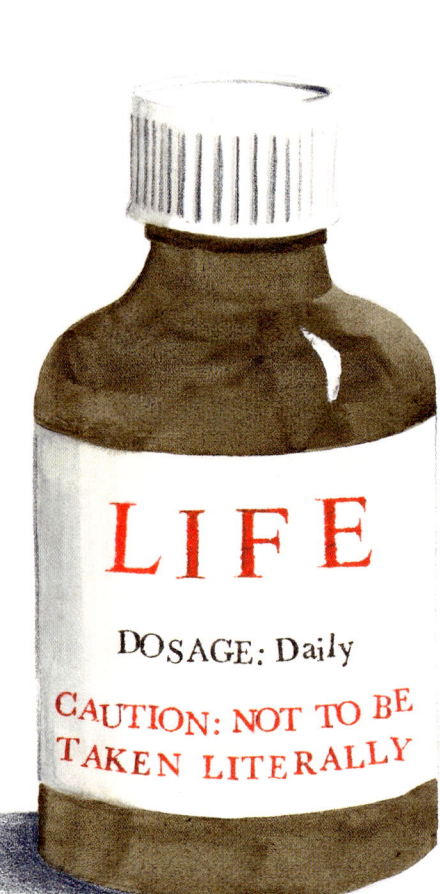

Yesterday, all my troubles
seemed so far away

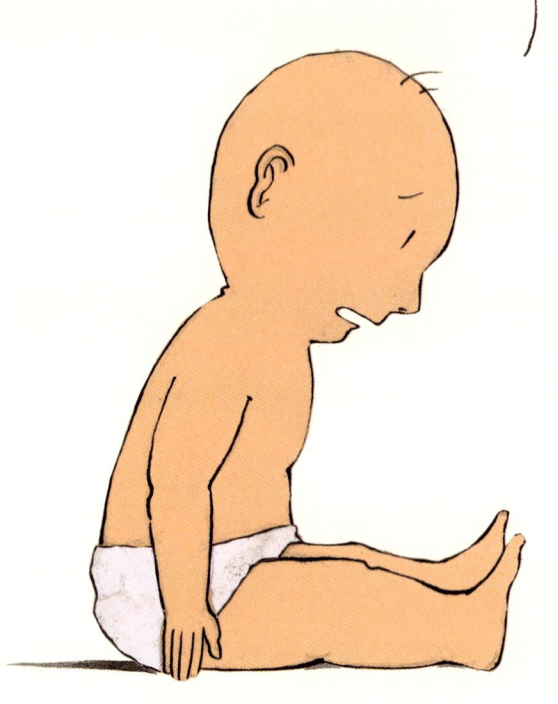

laid back          seriously
                   laid back

# LOST CAT

**Black and white male, answers to Jerry.**

I couldn't get a bed at the hospital, so I ended up at the veterinary hospital down the road ...

# Bird of Paradox

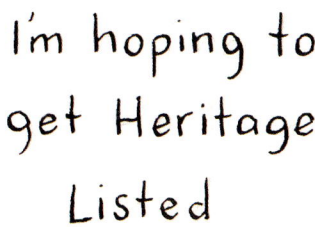

Edam & Yves

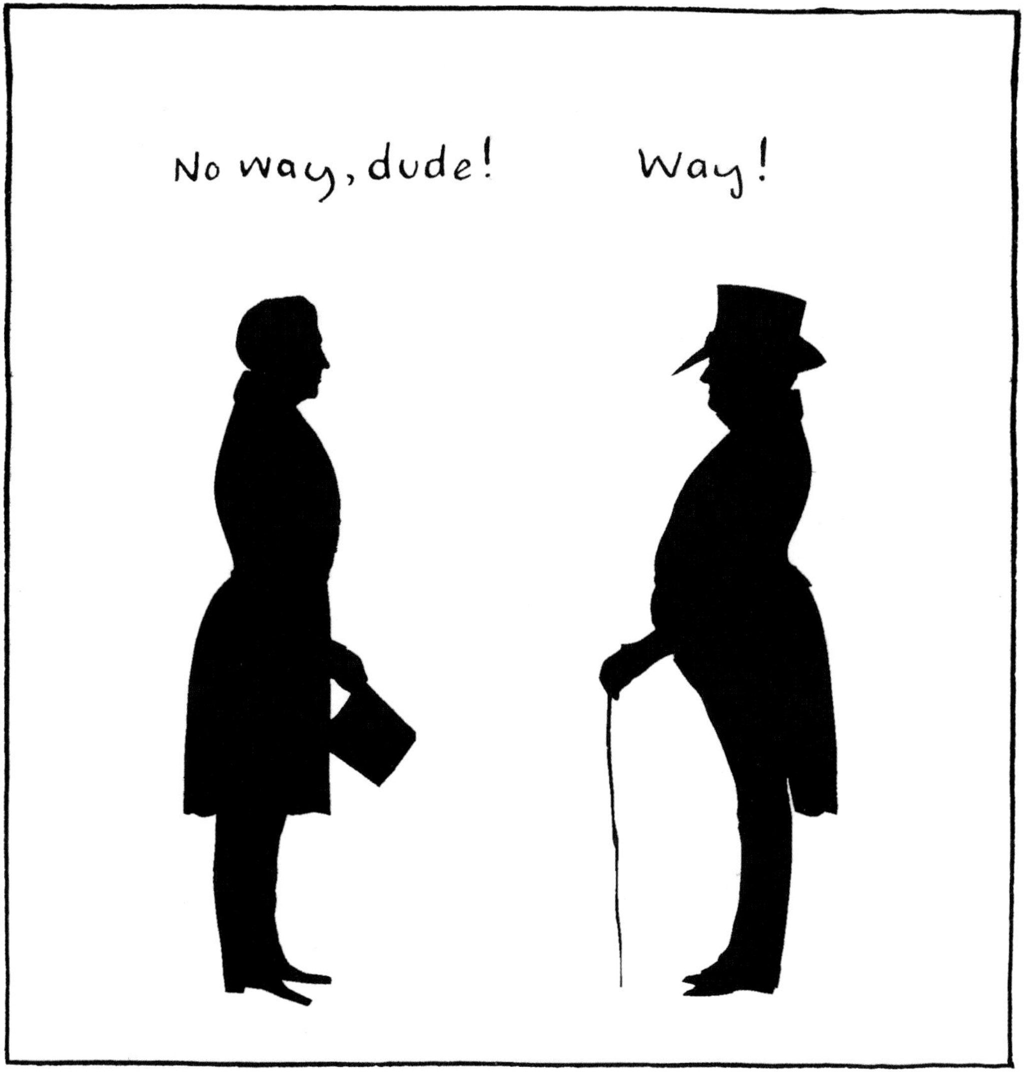
No way, dude!
Way!

# ST RAY of HOPE

Now I feel even worse!

That's because I'm a reverse psychologist

# EVERY DAG HAS HIS DAY

My goal is to
become incredibly
underrated

Problem is, the selfish part of me has become all generous and kind, and the considerate part of me has become really quite mean...

THE HOBBY MAKETH THE MAN

The North Sea is choppy
The Atlantic Ocean rolls
The Pacific Ocean ripples
The Dead Sea scrolls

I guess it's hard to know what to make of a sunset when you don't know its market value

# LITTLE CATERPILLAR

Little caterpillar
remember:
build wings
in this world
that you may fly
in the next.

# THE BIG BIG LITTLE THINGS

The <u>straw</u> that broke the camel's back

The <u>fly</u> in the ointment

The last <u>nail</u> in the coffin

The <u>thorn</u> in one's side

# BREAKFAST AT TIFFANY'S

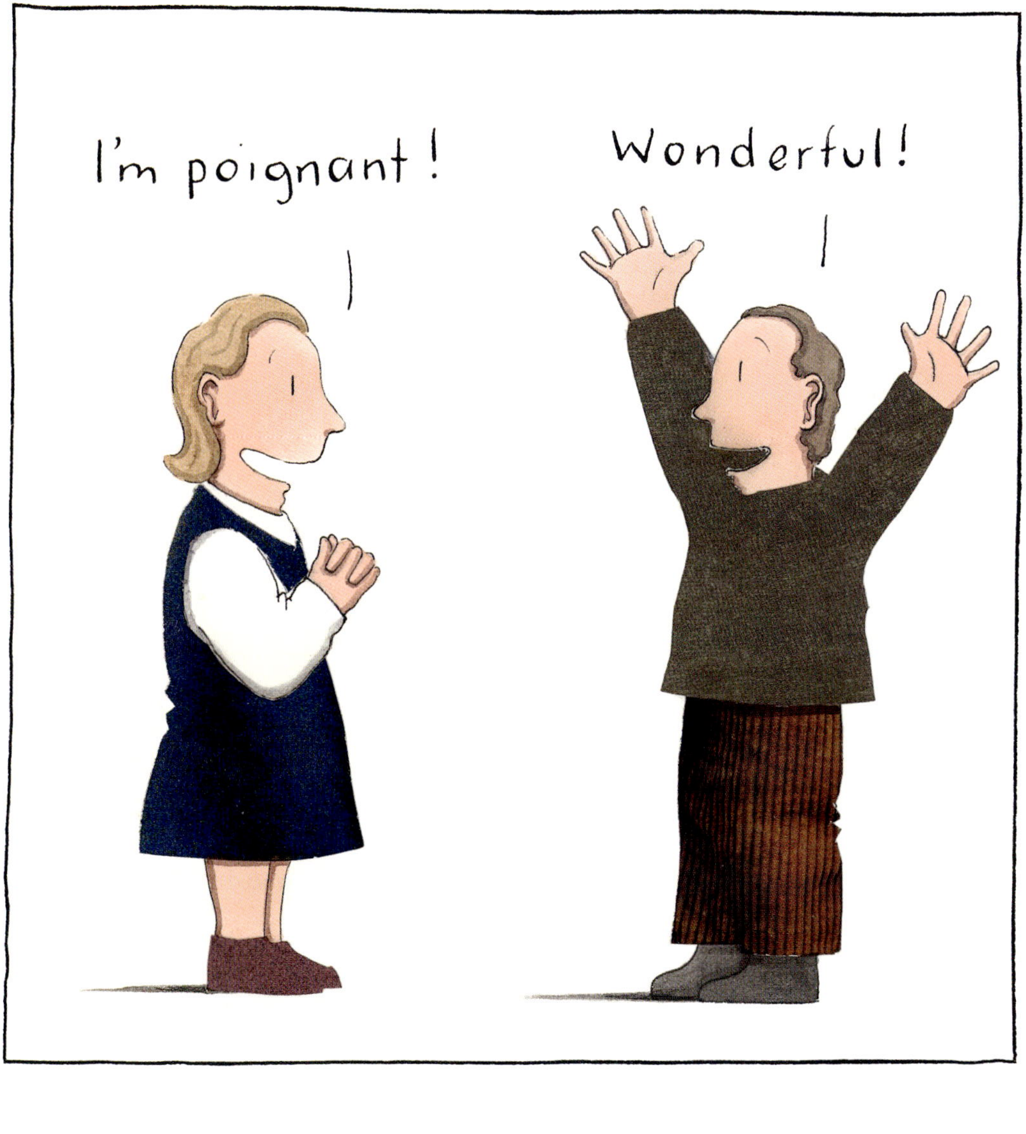
I'm poignant!
Wonderful!

# BLACK DOG

LOST AND FOUND

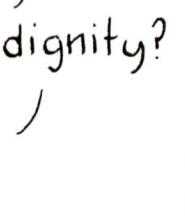

Do you recall when you lost your dignity?

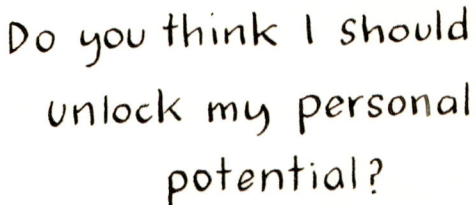

He tried to drown his sorrows
lamentably oblivious
to the little-known fact
that sorrows are amphibious.

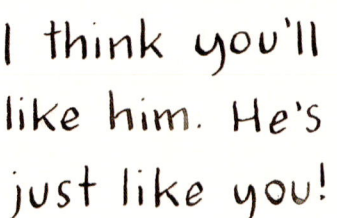

But you took him
by the left leg and
threw him down
        the stairs!

Nothing
Goosey Goosey
Gander hasn't
done

**Tohby Riddle** is the creator of numerous cartoons and picture books. *Pink Freud* is his second collection of cartoons. The cartoons first appeared before a wide audience in *Good Weekend* – the weekend magazine of the *Sydney Morning Herald* and Melbourne's *Age*. His cartoons have also been exhibited in the National Museum of Australia, Museum Victoria, and on a varied assortment of refrigerators.

His picture books include *Irving the Magician, The Singing Hat,* and *The Great Escape from City Zoo* – all shortlisted for the CBC Picture Book of the Year – and the cult favourite, *The Royal Guest.*

Tohby Riddle's previous cartoon collection is called *What's the Big Idea?*

www.tohby.com

PENGUIN BOOKS

Published by the Penguin Group
Penguin Group (Australia)
250 Camberwell Road
Camberwell, Victoria 3124, Australia
(a division of Pearson Australia Group Pty Ltd)
Penguin Group (USA) Inc.
375 Hudson Street, New York, New York 10014, USA
Penguin Group (Canada)
90 Eglinton Avenue East, Suite 700,
Toronto ON M4P 2Y3, Canada
(a division of Pearson Penguin Canada Inc.)
Penguin Books Ltd
80 Strand, London WC2R 0RL, England
Penguin Ireland
25 St Stephen's Green, Dublin 2, Ireland
(a division of Penguin Books Ltd)
Penguin Books India Pvt Ltd
11, Community Centre, Panchsheel Park, New Delhi-110 017, India
Penguin Group (NZ)
67 Apollo Drive, Rosedale, North Shore 0632, New Zealand
(a division of Pearson New Zealand Ltd)
Penguin Books (South Africa) (Pty) Ltd
24 Sturdee Avenue, Rosebank, Johannesburg 2196, South Africa

Penguin Books Ltd, Registered Offices: 80 Strand, London WC2R 0RL, England

First published by Penguin Group (Australia), a division of Pearson Australia Group Pty Ltd, 2007

1 3 5 7 9 10 8 6 4 2

Text and illustrations copyright © Tohby Riddle, 2007

Text and cover design by Megan Baker © Penguin Group (Australia)
Illustrations by Tohby Riddle
Typeset in Baker Signet Regular
Printed in Singapore by Imago Productions

National Library of Australia
Cataloguing-in-Publication data:

Riddle, Tohby.
Pink Freud.

ISBN 978 0 14 300767 8

1. Caricatures and cartoons. I. Title.

741.569

penguin.com.au